In the Jungle

ACTIVITY BOOK

Quarto is the authority on a wide range of topics.
Quarto educates, entertains, and enriches the lives of our readers—
enthusiasts and lovers of hands-on living.
www.quartoknows.com

Illustrated by Constanza Basaluzzo

6 Orchard Road, Suite 100
Lake Forest, CA 92630
quartoknows.com
Visit our blogs at quartoknows.com

Printed in Guangdong, China
1 3 5 7 9 10 8 6 4 2

FSC
www.fsc.org
MIX
Paper from
responsible sources
FSC® C101537

Table of Contents

Types of Jungle Animals

Tiger

One of the largest cats around, tigers are found in South and Southeast Asia.

A tiger usually eats about 15–35 pounds of meat per feeding, dining on deer, pigs, cattle, monkeys, birds, reptiles, and even fish. And when it's really hungry, a tiger can eat up to 90 pounds of meat in one meal!

Hippopotamus

These large creatures have little round ears, bulging eyes, and thick gray skin. They can open their mouths very wide to show off their giant teeth.

Hippopotamus means "river horse" in Greek. Rather than swim, these huge mammals actually walk along the bottoms of lakes and rivers. To keep cool, hippos spend most of their days in rivers and lakes with their nostrils, eyes, and ears poking above the water.

Giraffe

The giraffe has a very long neck, tall legs, a pair of horns, and a wiry tail. The tallest land animal on earth, a male giraffe can reach 19 feet tall!

Male giraffes are called "bulls," female giraffes are called "cows," and baby giraffes are called "calves." Giraffes are surprisingly fast; they can run more than 30 miles per hour!

Crocodile

One of the largest reptiles on earth, the crocodile is a stealthy predator with thick, plated skin and a long snout full of sharp teeth.

Crocodiles spend most of their time in water, such as rivers, estuaries, and marshlands. As they swim, they keep most of their body hidden while their nostrils, ears, and eyes poke above the surface.

Lion

Dubbed "King of Beasts," the lion is a large, regal feline that lives in a pride (or group). Lions use their deep, distinct roar to define their pride's territory.

Adult male and female lions look quite a bit different from each other. A male lion has a large mane around its head and neck and is much larger, sometimes weighing hundreds of pounds more than a female.

Rhinoceros

The rhinoceros is a huge, thick-skinned mammal with three toes on each foot. African rhinoceroses have two fibrous horns, which can grow up to 5 feet long.

The word rhinoceros comes from the Greek words *rhino* (meaning "nose") and *keras* (meaning "horn").

Crocodile Quest

Can you help this crocodile find the way to the water?

START

FINISH

Answer on page 40.

Spot the Difference

One of these frogs is different from the rest.
Can you tell which one?

Answer on page 40.

Jungle Time!

Can you name these animals?

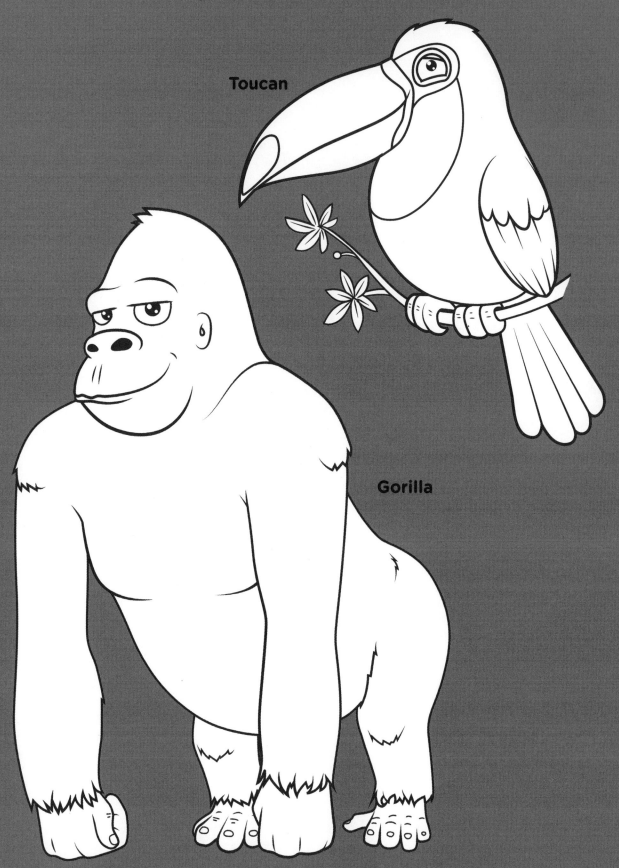

Toucan

Gorilla

Giraffe

Parrot

13

Draw a Monkey

Follow the steps to draw a monkey.

Give the monkey two arms, two legs, and a tail. Next draw a tuft of hair, facial features, and finish the ears.

Jungle Scene

Use markers to fill in the scene below.

Answer on page 40.

Spot the Difference

One of these parrots is different from the rest.
Can you tell which one?

Answer on page 40.

Draw a Toucan

Follow the steps to draw a toucan.

**Draw the toucan's feet and the branch.
Add his blue eye and yellow chest,
and fill in his beak.**

Jungle Time!
Can you name these animals?

Rhinoceros

Lion

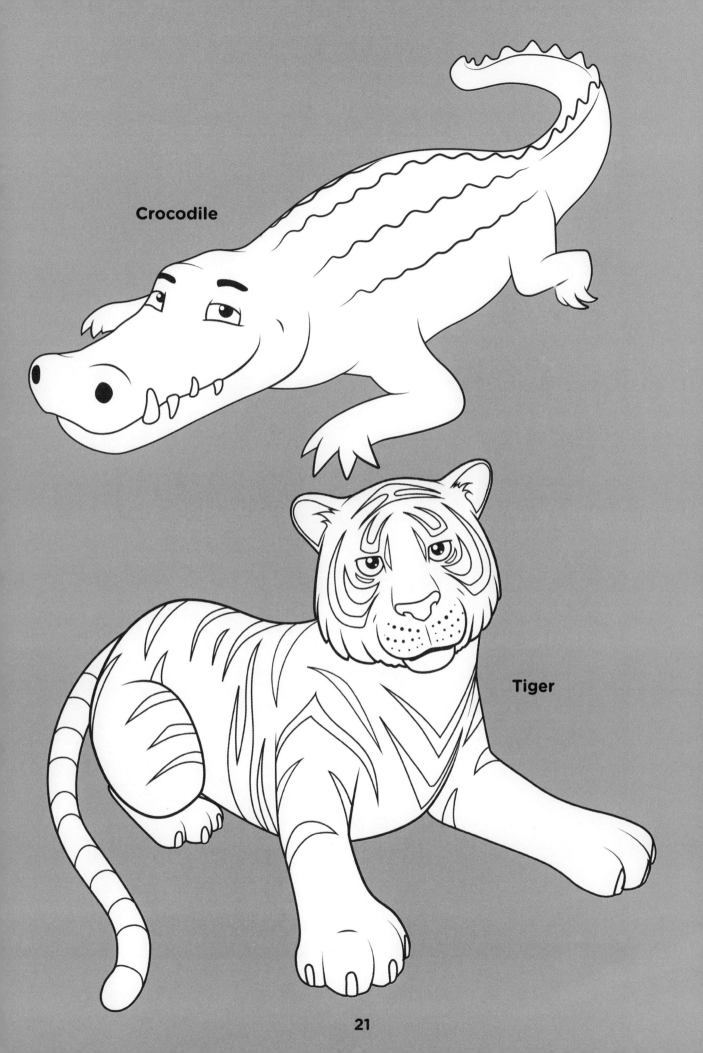

Crocodile

Tiger

Butterfly Quest

Help the explorer find the butterfly.

FINISH

START

Answer on page 40.

Spot the Difference

One of these leopards is different
from the rest. Can you tell which one?

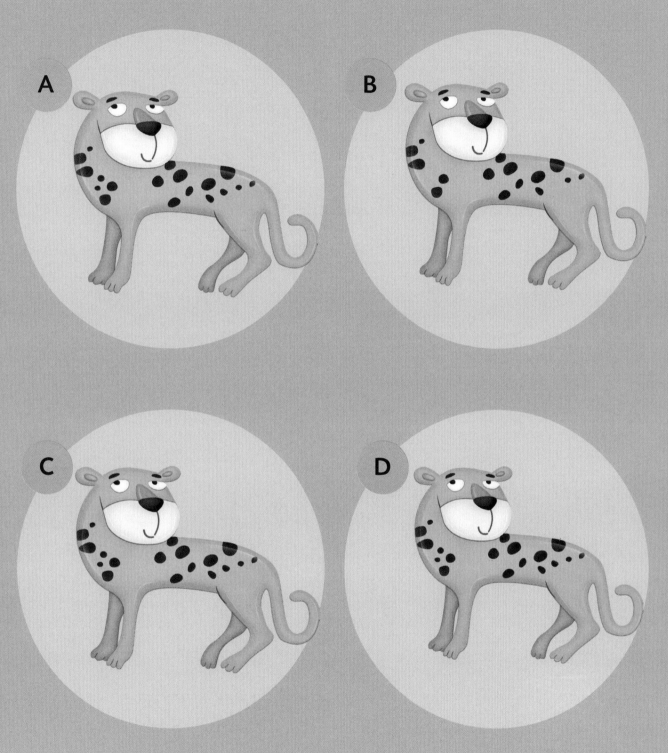

Answer on page 40.

Jungle Scene

Use crayons or markers to finish this jungle scene.

Dot-to-Dot

Follow the numbers on this dot-to-dot to reveal the animal.

Answer on page 41.

Draw a Lion

Follow the steps to draw a lion.

Draw the lion's head and body. Add his toes and a tuft of hair on his tail. Then add his eyes, nose, and smile.

Tic-Tac-Toe

Grab a friend and challenge them to a game!
Best of nine wins.

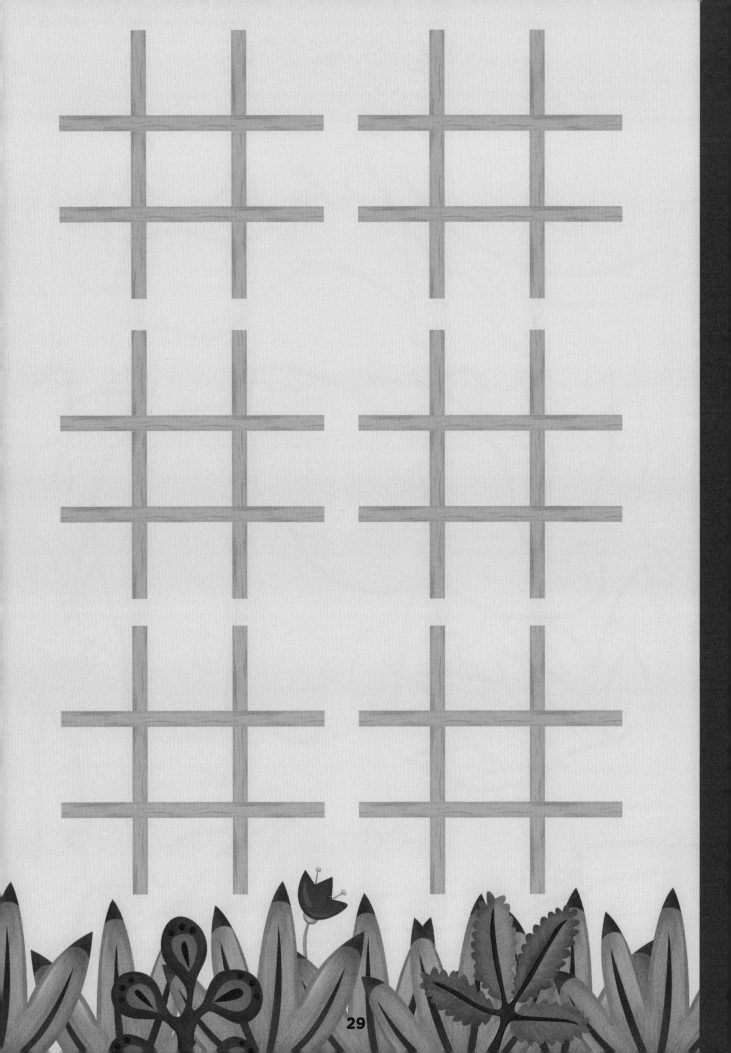

Jungle Scenes

Use crayons or markers to finish these jungle scenes.

Find the Bananas

This monkey loves bananas and is hungry.
Can you help him find the bananas?

START

FINISH

Answer on page 41.

Dot-to-Dot

Follow the numbers on this dot-to-dot to reveal the animal.

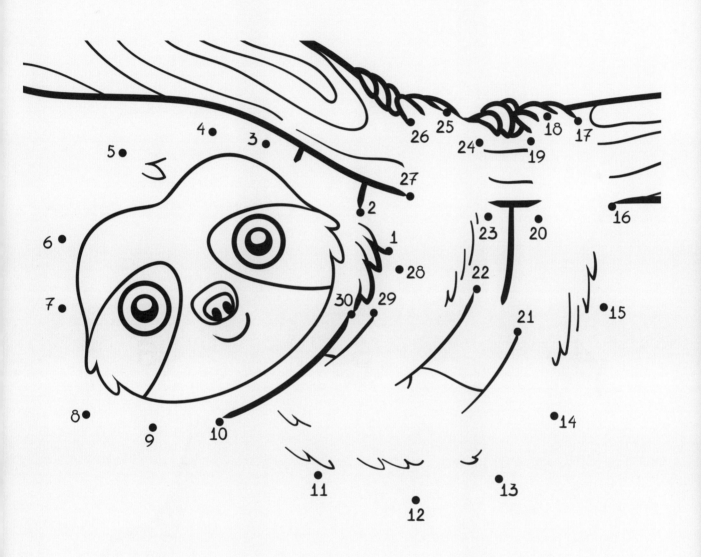

Answer on page 41.

Draw a Giraffe

Follow the steps to draw a giraffe.

Draw the giraffe's tail, ears, and horns. Add the mane and pattern, and draw a face and hooves.

Dot-to-Dot

Follow the numbers on this dot-to-dot to reveal the animal.

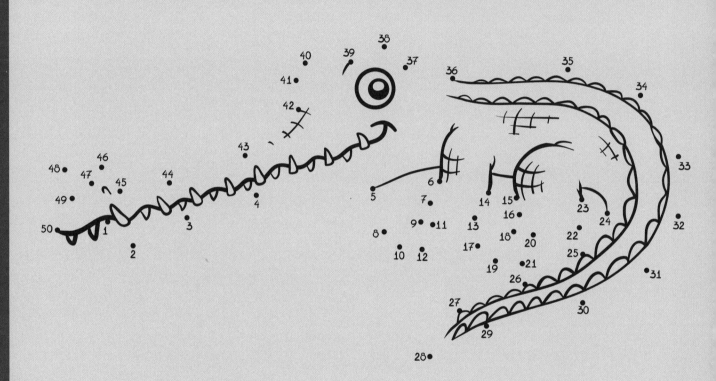

Answer on page 41.

Animal Quiz

Do you know the names of these animals?
Draw a line to the right word.

toucan

sloth

crocodile

leopard

iguana

frog

Answers on page 41.

Dot-to-Dot

Follow the numbers on this dot-to-dot to reveal the animal.

Answer on page 41.

On Safari!

Can you help this explorer find her way to the tiger?

START

FINISH

Answer on page 41.

Answer Key

Crocodile Quest
Page 10

Spot the Difference
Page 11

Jungle Scene
Page 16

Spot the Difference
Page 17

Butterfly Quest!
Page 22

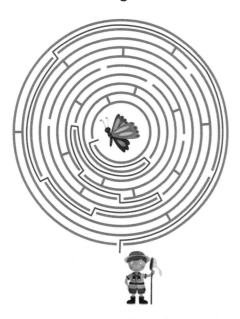

Spot the Difference
Page 23

Dot-to-Dot
Page 25

Find the Bananas
Page 32

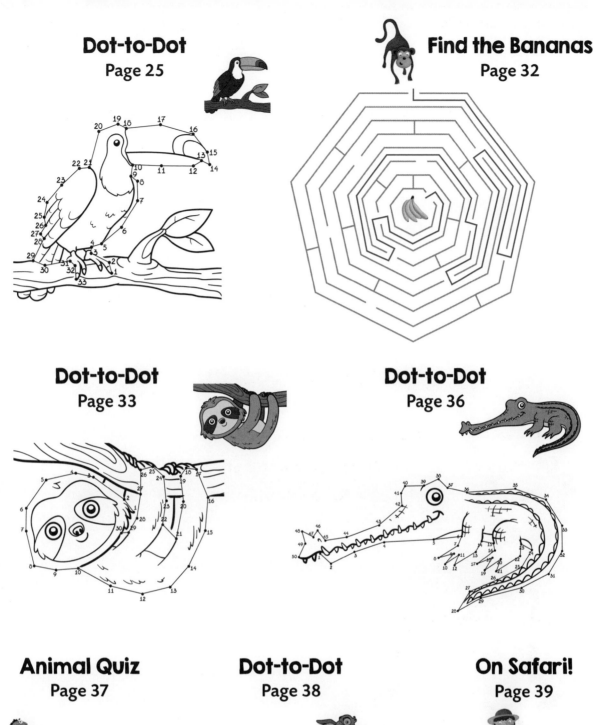

Dot-to-Dot
Page 33

Dot-to-Dot
Page 36

Animal Quiz
Page 37

toucan

sloth

crocodile

leopard

iguana

frog

Dot-to-Dot
Page 38

On Safari!
Page 39

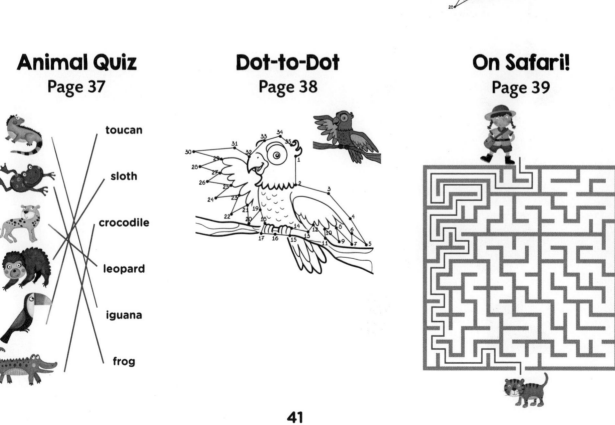

How to Play the Board Game

For 2 to 4 players

It's safari time! Who can race through the jungle and spot the most animals? Be the first player to complete the quest by landing on the safari complete space.

What you'll need:

• Game board

• A single die (not included)

• Explorer press-outs, one for each player

Each player picks an explorer press-out as their game piece and places it on the start space.

On your turn, roll the die to see how many spaces to move forward. Follow the directions of the space you land on.

Memory Game

For two or more players. Have a grown-up cut out the cards on the following pages to create a memory game.

To play, lay all the pieces facedown. Turn over one piece, and then another. If it is a match, put them to the side. If they don't match, turn them back over and let your opponent try. The player with the most matching pairs wins!

| bananas | bananas | blue bird |
| tiger | tiger | blue bird |

turtle

turtle

giraffe

toucan

toucan

giraffe

spider

spider

sloth

butterfly

butterfly

sloth

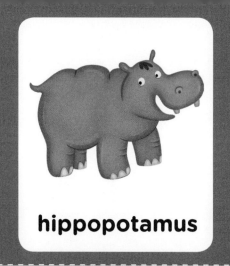

hippopotamus

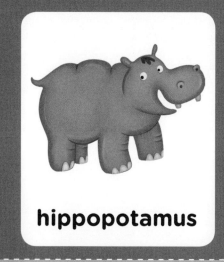

hippopotamus

tree

lion

lion

tree

explorer

explorer

rhinoceros

flamingo

flamingo

rhinoceros

Stickers and Press-out, Stand-up Figures

tiger cub

rhinoceros

tiger

hippopotamus

lion cub

lion

monkey

leopard

giraffe

crocodile